THEATER CRITICISMS

By Stanley Kauffmann

Novels

The Hidden Hero
The Tightrope
A Change of Climate
Man of the World

Criticism

THEATER

Persons of the Drama
Theater Criticisms

FILM

A World on Film
Figures of Light
Living Images
Before My Eyes

Editor

(With Bruce Henstell)
American Film Criticism: From the Beginnings to *Citizen Kane*

Memoirs

Albums of Early Life